Try!

A SURVIVAL GUIDE
TO
UNEMPLOYMENT

KAREN OKULICZ

K-Slaw, Inc.
P.O. Box 375
Belmar, NJ 07719

www.OKULICZ.com

Published by K-Slaw, Inc.
            P.O. Box 375
            Belmar, New Jersey 07719

Library of Congress Catalog Card Number: 94-96696

ISBN: 0-9644260-0-5

First Printing, January 1995
Second Printing, December 1995
Third Printing, July 1997
Fourth Printing, October 1997
Fifth Printing, June 1998
Sixth Printing, February 1998
Seventh Printing, December 1999
Eighth Printing, June 2000
Ninth Printing, November 2000
Tenth Printing, June 2001
Eleventh Printing, May 2002
Twelfth Printing, February 2003
Fourteenth Printing, February 2004
Fifteenth Printing, May 2004
Sixteenth Printing, February 2005

Printed in the United States of America

To my parents

Irene Olga Prostoff Okulicz
Joseph Paul Okulicz

Our greatest glory is not in never falling, but in rising every time we fall.

Confucius

Table of Contents

Introduction

This book is a practical and inspirational survival guide to unemployment. It will not teach you how to set up a resume or how to interview. What it will teach you is how to find out what you want to do and what you want to be; how to survive some basic aspects of unemployment pitfalls, along with tips on how to set up your work search process. The process is simple. All you have to do is . . .

1

Out of Work

It's probably not you, so get over that feeling it's your fault. If you were a clerical person, you probably were extremely competent. If a manager, a well respected leader. If a sales person, you probably made your quota and goals.

There is no rhyme or reason for the choice of who gets the axe. It might be a lack of performance or personality conflicts, but today it's just as likely to be financial or economic reasons much bigger than you, or your boss, or even your company.

But here goes the litany of words you'll hear: GOT THE AXE, MERGER, FIRED, DOWN-SIZED, LET GO, SHUT DOWNS, CANNED, or LAID OFF. Not so nice, huh? I was let go from two sales positions in a three-year period. I sold successfully in both positions. It didn't matter. I was let go. When your time is up, your time is up. You're let go because of "because." My first lay-off, I was told the company as a whole was not doing well. I was out of work for eleven months. Then I was hired elsewhere at the salary and territory I wanted. Five months later management changed. Five

3

months later, I was gone.

What was good about my second lay-off was that I had so much company within my own circle of friends. During my eleven months of my first search, I was the recipient of more than a few negative comments on the length of time I was out of work. They just had no idea about being unemployed! These comments came from people who were cocooned in corporations whose careers were secure....then. Now two of these people are out of work.

No matter who you are, how good a job you are doing, what level you're at, you are not safe from being unemployed. With so many changes in American businesses - like companies moving operations out of state or out of the country, buy-outs of companies or companies absorbing other companies, or changes in an industry or technology -- your lay-off is very seldom, if ever, a singular cause. So trust it's not you. It probably isn't.

2

Time

Wow! All that free time! You now have at least 45 extra hours a week. That is to say, if you worked a 40-hour week with a 15-minute commute. (Not many people I know have this schedule, but for illustration, I'll use 45 hours). For yourself, figure out your own commuting time and work schedule -- BINGO -- that equates to free time now. We could also go further and say most times we may be working on projects or conflicts when we're not at work. Like doing some work-related reading or discussing co-worker politics with a spouse or loved one. So, at 24 hours a day times seven days, you have 168 free hours a week. Wow! What now?

In the beginning, time on our hands is freeing and so relaxing. No meetings, no bosses, no structure, but no full-time paycheck! After a while it becomes a different kind of time. It drags and drags. Be aware of "rubber time" -- what used to take you an hour to accomplish when you were working, now can drag on or stretch out to three hours. As we look for employment, most of us -- to fill time -- naturally start those home projects that we never seemed to get to. During the project you may find out you're not good at the manual labor and don't like it.

Or you begin the sleep-late pattern as you look for employment. Sleeping late can be a sign of depression. It happens. Your job is to stay in a good mental state to overcome, subside or curb the depression.

It is very easy to forget what your purpose is. To be employed, the house projects or sleeping late are diversions from that purpose.

Structure your day from the start. Get up at the same time every day, if feasible. If you were commuting a long distance and got up an ungodly hour to commute, structure your day in a civilized manner. We all know our own time clocks. Seven o'clock wake-up time is fine to some, but not to others. There will be days that are endless hours for you. Some days it is not easy at times to keep up the pace of employment searching, volunteering, trying and exploring. There will be days that buying stamps for resumes may be all you can do as an accomplishment towards getting work. (It happens!) That's OK. You're still moving.

Use some of the time for healthy lifestyle changes in your life. This 45 extra hours a week is the best time to start that diet and/or exercise plan. There are no excuses about getting home late or a long commute, or road travel anymore. You will be clearer in your thinking and decision-making towards what you want to be and what you want to do. Even a little exercise has been known to increase one's ability to solve and process problems.

I did not do this my first time out. But it helped the second. I do not recommend getting laid off twice to learn to use this precious time wisely for positive lifestyle changes. Try it and you'll find out.

3

Cry, Cry, Cry

Yep, no matter how tall we grow, we cry! Do it. Do it privately, do it with a loved one, do it with a friend. It will make you feel better and the emotional release will spur you to move forward.

My first time out, I went through many, many emotions. Mostly, I was angry. Having worked so hard in helping to build a new business, I was confused and frustrated that my efforts did not pay off for me. I've come to learn that what seeds are planted today or experiences tried don't always manifest themselves until some time later in a different form. My experience with marketing that particular product are the same skills used to market this book. So let it go. It's time to move on. Plus you're out of work. There is no choice but to move forward.

To be honest, my first time laid off I sat paralyzed in fear the whole eleven months of my unemployment. I was terrified I was not going to work again at the level or money I needed. I sent out my resumé and did my follow-ups and interviewed, but I was afraid.

The second time I was much more directed with my

personal well-being. I knew how to look for work. Now I knew I had to look for me and at me to get myself happily employed. I exercised more, ate better, read everything positive, went to church and joined a meditation group. Again, don't wait till time two. *Use this time wisely now.*

If you have strayed from your religion, I recommend going back or finding a new one. It works. Period. Whatever you believe in, you do need it now and always, but especially now for direction. Go somewhere you'll be comfortable. I found an abbey nearby. I still am not clear as to when to stand, sit or kneel, but I watch around me.

Read everything positive. You will work again. I call inspirational literature vitamins for the soul. You know what is best for you. No need to purchase books. The library will have the right thing for you to read.

Stay with positive people. Negativity poisons productivity. We all know who pushes our negative buttons, so stay clear of those people. If you are surrounded by negativity from family or neighbors, set boundaries with time you spend with them and keep moving forward. You do not have the time to waste listening to anything negative. Negativity will breed self-doubt. We don't need these negative people to figure out what to do or who to be.

I admit, this is not easy. I had many tantrums over not wanting to go to an interview, type a cover letter, do a follow-up call or do this book. Have them, have them fast and move on.

If you feel you need more direction than you can give yourself at this time, look into available counseling. Your company may offer out-placement counseling. Your COBRA plan (if you have one) will handle mental health benefits. Or, see your clergy. Remember, you are the product which must remain as fresh as possible to sell.

The habits and discipline you learn now while you try, explore, volunteer, cry, may last a lifetime. The reason why is you have the time (hopefully not too long) to learn and face yourself. This is your gift of time to go forward in the best manner for the greatest good for yourself and those you love. Corny, huh? Maybe.

So go ahead. *Have a good cry.* It will make you feel better. This time is not forever.

4

Carry the Colander

Webster's definition of colander: A perforated pan for draining liquids. My definition of a colander: An object with holes in it to drain out what is not necessary and to save what is.

At any time, people around you will blurt out unsolicited advice -- *what* you should be doing, *how* you should be doing it, *when* you should be doing it, *where* you should be doing it, and *why* you should be doing it. This barrage of advice can seem endless. It takes a lot of patience not to scream "I'm working on looking for work. Leave me alone. Mind your own business." I do not need to tell you who you want to direct those statements to. You already know.

However, most times these people are trying to be helpful. It can be overwhelming in the beginning when you are so new and you really haven't a clue of what you're going to do, what you want to do, when you want to do it, where, or why. And it's hard to listen to advice when you've been out for a "while" and are at your wit's end with rejections and opportunities falling apart. Take people's questions and advice with a grain of salt.

BUT!

Listen -- because someone's observations of you may give you an insight of your hidden talents. Listen to what you've been telling yourself for years. I hate to drive or commute over an hour. I hate wearing a suit, etc. You know what is best for you. Other people's comments will offer insights. Just carry the colander!

5

What Do You Want to Do?

I believe the "thing" we are or do can be broken down into three categories: a job, a career, or a life's work.

Definitions:

A Job: Something to pay the bills. A job you take until you finish school, or apprenticeship, or whatever. It helps to cover expenses. It may be mentally or physically demanding, but its rewards are financial only. It gets us by. It's doin' what you gotta do to get through.

A Career: Something you go to school for, training or apprenticeship. A specialty, a trade. You may be in a career because you felt you may like it or it was suggested to you. It may be challenging for you, but you think there could always be something better. You may like your career and are comfortable with the choice, but will be glad to retire someday.

A Life's Work: AH! The pinnacle of all employment! To do something you love. To have a passion for the thing you do. To lose yourself in this work totally. The rewards may not be financial, but may be pure joy.

Example: the musician that plays free of charge. A career can be a life's work, but a job will never become a life's work.

Most people have been working for many years and because of their life commitments or fears they stay in their jobs or careers, not very happy at all. This unemployment may be the time to switch from a job to a career or to your life's work.

Unemployment does not differentiate between sex, age, race, marital status or sexual orientation. When you are unemployed, that's it -- out of work -- end of story! You are no longer a full functioning salesperson, computer operator, waitress, truck driver, or CEO. You were. It's in the past. Now, you are one nebulous thing. You are UNEMPLOYED. So being this one thing you really are faced with, the only thing you have left which is yourself.

This change of status from working to not working is one of the most personal and devastating experiences we can face as individuals. No one else experiences the loss of status as dramatically as we do. And with these times, we may never be able to return to what we were doing.

Now we have to figure out what we want to do, what we want to be -- and a step further -- why we want to be the thing we choose.

6

Find
The Treasure

Most of us are so comfortable about making a list of options we need when buying a car, or the necessities we are looking for in a house while house hunting. Well, now it's time to make the list about us for employment hunting. It's an uncomfortable task to do because it is a soul-searching process that most of us are not used to doing. We have been so busy being busy. Than to, examine our employment needs. We all have needs in this area -- likes and dislikes -- that we face every day. We like the work, but we do not like who we are working for. Or we hate the commute. It's a combination of many items that make up working needs. By doing and being what we want to be and do we will be happier. Being happy makes you a better neighbor, friend, husband, wife, parent and child. A better world no doubt.

The list is a Wish List that gets worked as you search for the buried treasure. The mystery of *you* evolves as you gather the clues towards the treasure.

To begin, keep the Wish List private. The reason is not to open yourself up to criticism, especially in the beginning of the process. The Wish List you start in the beginning changes over time as you change through the soul-searching, interviewing, exploring, etc. I shared my first Wish List with loved ones to be asked months down the line, "Well, what about join-ing the circus? You didn't leave yet?" Umm. Not shar-ing so fast saves on the aggravation of discussion that is unnecessary until you are solid with your direction. This is your Wish List. Not someone's Wish List for you or of you!

Once you've refined it, the Wish List will keep you clear as you go to interviews and help guide you with questions to ask an interviewer. It keeps you directed to what you want, or close to it. Let's begin to gather the clues toward the treasure.

Your Personal Wish List

Here are some clues to get you started. Fill in the appropriate answers, and at the end sum it all up. You'll know what you're looking for.

HOW WILL YOU GET TO THIS NEW PLACE?
By car, bus, train, plane?

_____

_____

HOW FAR AWAY WILL THIS NEW PLACE BE?
An hour away, a half-hour away? Take a protractor, yes
a protractor, and circle the area surrounding your
home on the maximum mileage you would want to
commute. (My father's practical rule of thumb.)

_____

WHAT WILL THIS NEW PLACE LOOK LIKE?
A tall office building, a field of grass? Ummm. A
cubicle, a trailer, a factory, a home?

_____

_____

_____

WHO WILL BE THERE? Lots of people? What kind?
Men or women or a mixture?

_____

_____

_____

SHOULD THERE BE A RELIGIOUS
PREFERENCE?

_____

WHO DO YOU REPORT TO? BE HONEST. THIS
IS YOU. What kind of chemistry is there? You'll know
when you get to the interview and are being interviewed by a particular boss if you feel comfortable.

_____

_____

WHAT TIME DO YOU GO THERE? Nine to five, flex time, shift work? You know your time clock -- what works best for you?

_____

WHAT WILL YOU BE WEARING? A suit, casual wear, a uniform, a hat and a name tag?

_____

_____

MORE ON TIME & PLACE: WOULD YOU RELO-CATE? Can you handle night meetings, or weekend work? Who watches the pets, kids, plants, tropical fish if you're late or have to travel? If there was always a place you wanted to move to, this may be the time to move.

_____

_____

_____

WILL YOU FIT IN SUCH A PLACE, OR DO YOU CREATE THE PLACE TO FIT YOU? Do consulting work instead of being a full-time employee?

_____

_____

WHAT ARE YOUR SKILLS? Do you need more schooling? Do you like a hobby that could be a life's work? Are your skills transferable?

_____

_____

_____

HAVE YOU DAY-DREAMED ABOUT SUCH A PLACE?

_____

_____

WHAT WILL YOU GET WHEN YOU GET THERE? Accomplishment, satisfaction, fame, riches, status, love, recognition.

_____

HOW WILL YOU GET PAID? Lottery payments? (Oops!) Weekly, monthly?

_____

WHAT WILL THE SALARY RANGE BE? Will there be a dental plan, a medical plan, life insurance, sick time, vacation time, tuition reimbursement? How much? 401K, pension plan? Stock options?

_____

_____

_____

_____

WILL THEY PUT THINGS IN WRITING TO KEEP <u>ALL</u> HONEST???

These items should trigger you to make your own questions. This should be your Wish List. For example, by the time I figured my next career move in sales, I worked out details on territory and salary. One of the most important questions I have on my Wish List I ask at a closing interview is about commission. No cap on commission has always been a top priority to me. (Of course, sales people know how many times the company can change the sales plan later. Especially if you're selling well. Go figure! I never understood this.) Keep referring to your Wish List, deleting and adding. *Knowing what you don't want also brings you to what you do want.* Once you start the process, you'll be surprised how it uncovers the buried treasure which is you and what you want to do!

7

Try, Try, Try

OK. You now have at least forty-five free hours a week and some treasure map clues. This may be the one and only time to try something you have always wanted to do. Think about when you were working or commuting. Did you say to yourself "Boy, if I only had the time I'd try this or that. I couldn't do that I work during those hours." Well, now you have the time. I can't emphasize enough to *TRY, TRY, TRY*.

If you are collecting unemployment and find a small job you may be worried about losing benefits. WHY? Each state is different. Check your local office or, if collecting out of state, check with the state you are collecting from. Some states allow you to make a small amount of wages and still collect.

However, I suggest volunteering. If you always wanted to do work in a florist, go to your local floral shop and ask if you can observe. You may find that you really don't like it. Or you may find that you do. Maybe you can work part-time and build it into something bigger.

My first time out of work I volunteered in a travel

agency. I had been a flight attendant and, having traveled a lot, I thought I'd be a natural as a travel agent. Wrong. I found it wasn't for me. It wasn't enough out and about that I was used to as a salesperson. Too much inside office time.

My second time out of work, I was much more proactive. (Again, do not wait to get laid off twice before you use some of this books' techniques.) My first time out of work I sat in fear that I was not going to work again. My second time I knew I would work; I just didn't know when. Plus, I was looking to be happy. I knew I wanted a quality of life that fit me as an individual.

How did I go about this by trying, trying, trying? I live near the beach and always daydreamed how it would be nice to have a little ice cream stand. Well, I knew some people who had one in a different town and asked if they needed summer help. I had visions of nice, easy days or nights scooping ice cream. Easy? Never! I now know why you see 15 and 16 year olds scooping ice cream. I have arthritis in both hands which flares up in the winter months. I never dreamed that scooping ice cream would trigger it. Well, after a few evenings of scooping, I would wake up with claw hands.

The whole experience of ice cream scooping lasted 20 hours tops. My ice cream business was never going to happen.

I then stopped in to see an old client in the food business, who I had once sold a financial program. I told him I was unemployed, again. We were chatting and he told me he was having a problem with his coleslaw vendor. I loudly heard opportunity knocking. So I said to him -- "I can make coleslaw." He said, "OK. Let's try it." Well, now my mind is working. Great. I see it now! K-Slaw, Inc. I would have a jingle like "K-slaw-slaw. What ever will be, will be." It was big. I went home and made a coleslaw portion for four. I brought my product back and had my friend try it. Well, it was a bit salty. But, he dragged out a 30-gallon tub of coleslaw and said, "This is the portion I need every few days." Now it's back to the arthritic hands. I was never going to be able to chop, mix, dice or stir 30 gallons of coleslaw!

This business venture lasted the time it took to make a portion of coleslaw for four. I did, however, use the name K-Slaw, Inc. This book was published by K-Slaw, Inc.

I knew now I had an entreé (small pun) into the food business. What did I make that family and friends ever commented on? (This is the listening technique. Carry the colander.) Peanut Butter Brownies! I did make K's PB Brownies once a week for my friend's place. After two weeks I was asked to make chocolate chip brownies. So K's CC Brownies were born. I don't have a jingle at this time, but I'm working on it.

What this little business taught me was how to unit-price my time, materials, ingredients, etc. A small start into something bigger?

How did I start to do this book? A couple of things led me to do this. Friends would call and say they had been laid off and didn't have a clue where to begin, what to do, what to set up, or how to look for what was available to them. They would ask how I did it. Why did it take so long for the search. I would tell them about the realities of interviewing and how some weeks are packed with opportunities and others are just a desert of time.

First, I'd say, take advantage of any outplacement your company offers you. Even if it's a phone and a desk to get you started. Phone bills can be expensive. Go to your local library to do research. Some organizations meet for networking. Check your local paper for a particular organization and ask about career opportunities. Use all the FREE services available that you can; you just don't know how long you will be out of work. *Network, network, network!* I've heard some executives say there are no possibilities in the newspaper. Wrong. I've found small companies starting up will advertise this way. Start with a new company. This could mean stock options from sweat equity. You have to try everything. The goal is to be employed and at best happily employed. So let's TRY, TRY, TRY. Utilize headhunters and employment agencies, or volunteer at a company you may want to work for or an industry you want to be in. How about old clients or vendors, or prospects you dealt with in your last position? Would you want to work for them or with them? Start your own business? My local community college has lots of videos on how to start all kinds of businesses. If you can afford it, go back to school for more skills. Take a job to support this effort. I always waitressed during my undergraduate and graduate school time. I couldn't even think about it now. Darn those fingers!

Your objective is to be working. With these times, you may not be able to go back to what you were once doing. So TRY, TRY, TRY. Everything. Something will appear that will be to your liking and will fit you. I guarantee it will be a pleasant surprise. So go ahead, just TRY.

8

The Unemployment Juggle

Now that you are trying, trying, trying, how do you keep track of all this activity?

The unemployment juggle is exhausting. To work is a lot easier than to look for work. I have set up a grid that tracks your activities on a weekly basis. There is a sample to get you started.

My first lay-off I sent out 978 resumes. I filled five notebooks of 70 pages each on search data. Company information/classified ads, leads. The system I used to keep track of my activity was quite simple. I would cut an ad out of the newspaper and tape it to the left side of a page and number the ad or the incoming idea. (Let's say a friend told me to call so-and-so. That would get jotted in the notebook with a number assigned to it.) The top of the pages were dated. When a call would come in or a rejection letter received, I would refer back to the number item and write next to it what the activity was (i.e., an interview, the date of the interview and the time of the interview), or if I received a rejection letter, what the response was.

Get all local newspapers for classified ads. Use Business Opportunity Listings for business ideas.

SAMPLE-SAMPLE-AMPLE-SAMPLE
WEEKLY DAY GUIDE

Time	MON.	TUES.	WED.	THURS.	FRI.
8 am	Exercise	Morning Walk	Exercise	Visit Out-placement Center	Exercise
9 am	Review Classified Ads	**Interview**	Make Follow-Up Phone Calls		Breakfast with former co-worker to network
10 am	Set Up Data Notebook	Library Research			
11 am	↓	Join local business organization (free)	Work on Notebook	↓	Library Research
12 pm	Healthy Lunch	Healthy Lunch	**Lunch Interview**	Volunteer at Local Deli to see if you want to buy one	Healthy Lunch
1 pm	Send Out Resumes	Make Follow-Up Phone Calls	Free Afternoon Have Fun		
2 pm					
3 pm	↓		↓		**Got The Call**
4 pm					Got a Job Celebrate
5 pm		↓		↓	**New Work!** Reward
6 pm					**yourself,** buy something new but inexpensive!

49

SAMPLE DATA PAGE:

Ad/Lead	Date	Response/Outcome
#101- NY Timely News Manager Wanted	Sent Resume 1/1	Received call 2/1 requesting interview. Interview set for 2/7 - 10 am
#102 - Headhunter Joe Joes	Called 2/4 with lead (Phone #...)	Has 2 opportunities One great - Second not for me
#103 - Called my Brother Paul for info on Company XYZ	Date Called: 2/5	Not hiring now. Recall 2 months

REMINDER:
Keep track of every letter and call.

A number of resumes sent or calls made were never responded to. Separately, I set up a grid with the categories I wanted to keep track of: opportunities pending, opportunities rejected by me or them. The first time out of work I rejected 11 offers (salary, territory or product was of no interest). I had 70 face-to-face interviews, 80 over the phone. Countless rejection calls and letters. I would tally weekly to see how I was doing. What was I being faced with? Not the right salary or product? During this time of unemployment, employers didn't return phone calls. There were just too many people out of work and not enough opportunities. However, I would try my best to follow through to get answers. Remember, you are not their priority at this time, unless the company is being pressured to hire. There will be interviews that you may go on that never hire anyone for that position. Lack of manners is unbelievable! Keep going. Your job is to get work. Make that follow-up call. Send that Thank You note. No matter how bad you felt about the company or the person you interviewed with THIS IS A SMALL WORLD AND A LONG LIFE. The people you may interview with may remember you for something else in the future. Or they may tell someone about you.

Keep a separate log on each interview so you have the information to keep track of what was said or offered. How did you feel? Most importantly, were you comfortable with the situation? Would you work there with them? Check your Wish List.

Keep a dream section in your notebook of ideas you get while daydreaming. Ideas while daydreaming may trigger more clues on what you should be doing.

Keep an accounting page of expenses. Keep track of mileage and tolls to the interview. Keep track of the cost of resumes, paper, envelopes, stamps, receipts, office supplies, faxes and thank you notes. This search is tax deductible.

Keep every rejection letter. Why? Because you don't know what you may be selling or who you may be working for or with. You may need an entry later into the company you interviewed with. Every rejection letter has a name or a contact at that company, a company address, and a company phone number. You may be able to use this for a mailing list someday.

Let's say you had a face-to-face interview. They didn't hire you but, now you have a face with a name to use in the future. The point is, the corporate world is changing employees rapidly. (Don't we know that!). If you stay with the same industry, you keep running into the same people. The oddest things can happen. That awful boss you had two years ago may be your employee tomorrow. Interesting thought!

9

Don't Stop Living Stop Spending

You may have received severance, vacation pay, bonus pay, a commission check, and then you may be going on unemployment. Stop spending. You never know how long you may be out of work, and you may need every dime to support yourself and your family. If you've been lucky enough to have made great money and saved it, you may have a cushion to get you through to the next full-time paycheck. Most of us are not that fortunate.

Funny how, awhile ago, you'd hear financial analysts say how one must keep three months savings for living expenses if you get laid off. Now that time has grown. The search process can take a very long time and it is costly to look for work. The cost of resumes, phone calls, car expense, travel expense, office supplies, faxes, etc.

I once worked with a woman who brought her lunch everyday to work even though there was a subsidized cafeteria available. Every February she went to the Caribbean partially funded on the savings of the home-made lunches. Not a bad thing.

However, this is not about Caribbean vacations.

This is all and all out big league budgeting for sure. Clip coupons for food. See if there are double coupons in your area. Rent movies or go to matinees. Eat at home. Go to garage sales. Arrangements can sometimes be made on outstanding bills (dentists, medical, telephone, utilities, credit cards, etc.) if you are unemployed. Call your creditors and find out what can be worked out. Plus network with them, too. They may need someone like you for their company. You never know. You must ask.

Spend money on a new suit for the interview? What if you land a position that you aren't going to need a suit? Save your money! You probably have something you can wear. You just don't know how long you will be looking. If you have a special occasion to go to, borrow, rent or go to a consignment shop. Being unemployed without a full-time paycheck is quite the test of budgeting.

Keep a running log for a week or two on your daily cash spending. There are always places to save money. The dimes and nickels add up.

10

Interviewing: The Front Line

Having sold for 15 years, I've had more than enough experience with meeting new people, either clients or prospects. Selling every day to new prospects is like being interviewed. I represented not only myself, but my product or service. Over the course of time, I've had about 2,000 appointments. So I can say I'm pretty savvy at interviewing. Well --- Yes and No!

As part of past training, I once spent some time with a senior saleswoman who I learned much from. She had the best sales style, mixed with a very accurate and deadly close. (A close in sales means you made the sale!) Anyway, she turned to me on the day's start and said that no matter how good you are, you could go into a presentation and start talking Pig Latin -- a language that you, the client or prospect does not understand. Don't take it for granted, she told me, that you can't have a bad day and just be off. Days you forget your resume or simply a pen. Just know it's not always or forever. With 70 face-to-face interviews, I had quite a few "talking Pig Latin" days.

I was at the Grand Hyatt in New York interviewing

with the President and Council of a Managed Care Company. I was on, I was exact, I knew my stuff. I was negotiating supremely. It was a breakfast meeting and the restaurant was full. The meeting was at a close. We were getting up to shake hands. I forgot I was seated on a small couch. Probably forgot because I was preoccupied with how brilliant I was at the moment. Well, I kept moving along the couch, proceeded to slip off and fall, legs straight in the air for all the world to see. Nice, huh? Never got the position! They must have felt I was brilliant, but with a lack of common sense.

Then there was the time on a closing interview I had to meet with top-of-all top sales managers for a final approval. I looked down at myself in the reception area and noticed I had two different suit pieces on! The suit jacket did not in any stretch of the imagination match the skirt. I must have pulled out of the closet these pieces from two different blue suits. Very different blues, very different fabric. I'm on the way into the meeting. There is nothing I could do. I was ushered into the conference room to wait for this top of all top managers. So I sat myself opposite the door.

When he arrived, I stood with my brief case in front of me to hide the skirt and jacket clash. After shaking hands, I sat down and wedged myself as far under the conference table as possible, short of cutting off breathing. I did get the position!

The point is, no matter how good you are, you WILL have the days of disasters. Be kind to yourself. This is not always or forever.

11

You!

This unemployment is not only about the work search, it is about YOU! The multiple facets of you that go into working. How you dress for work, how you get there, what you do, who you're with, etc. Your likes and dislikes, your values. The search is not an easy one. Be kind to yourself. This may be the life-trigger that was meant to happen -- your chance to fulfill yourself. Be kind to yourself and let others be kind to you. One friend would always ask me to come over in the late afternoon to visit when I was unemployed and then invite me for dinner. Her way of making my life in some way easier. I noticed it was a nice thing to do. Thanks, Clem.

Give up the anger and do things without malice. Once, I left behind a long list of sales leads at a company I helped build. The person who replaced me never contacted what was a wealth of possible business. No one is you. No one has your style. No one can take the place of your uniqueness. So let it go. Redirect your uniqueness to do its best for you and others.

LISTEN and BELIEVE in your instincts. I was

very close to closing an offer with a medical laboratory. I had three interviews and was just not comfortable with myself over the interviews. In fact, after every interview, I would get a bad headache. I thought it was the fumes from the laboratory. Well, I accepted the offer to start. Then I received an employment contract in the mail. The company was never up front about this contract during the interview process. I'm at this point with two month's mortgage to pay. I was uncomfortable and refused to sign.

Two months later, I got a position with 30% more to start and a better territory. Keep remembering your instincts. There are some places you don't belong - and people you don't belong with. Period. Rule of thumb: how do you feel when you initially leave that place or that person? Those are the feelings to pay attention to. They will tell all.

Think of this time to be personal and precious. Take stock, reflect on what will make you happy. Use the time to begin to exercise and diet. Keeping your basic responsibilities and life commitments, of course. This time is for you to process all you learned through trying, crying, prospecting, listening, interviewing, juggling and living to find that job that helps get you the career or the hobby just waiting to become a life's work. All the work to get to the work will bring you something to make you happily employed.

Just remember -- your direction may not be coleslaw, either. But you won't know until you've tried!

Good Luck!

About the Author

Karen Okulicz received a Bachelor of Science Degree from Fairleigh Dickinson University. She has had many, many jobs, a few careers, and is working towards her life's work.

"Try! A Survival Guide to Unemployment" is her first book.

Go to www.OKULICZ.com to read a chapter from her latest book **"Decide! How to make any Decision"**.

ORDER FORM

TO ORDER: "TRY! A SURVIVAL GUIDE TO UNEMPLOYMENT"
FIRST CHECK WITH YOUR LOCAL BOOKSTORE OR PLEASE
SEND

OF BOOKS _____ X $10.00 PER BOOK   = _____

        PLUS _____ X $.60 PER BOOK   = _____
                 NJ Sales tax if applicable

        PLUS _____ $2.50 SHIPPING & HANDLING = _____
                 PER BOOK

                 TOTAL ENCLOSED. = $ _____

          BULK DISCOUNTS AVAILABLE

MAKE CHECK OR MONEY ORDER PAYABLE TO K-SLAW, INC.,
P.O. BOX 375, BELMAR, NEW JERSEY 07719

PLEASE PRINT

NAME_____

ADDRESS_____

CITY_____STATE_____ZIP_____

THANK YOU!